Hymns for Young Pianists

Dedicated to all those parents and guardians who through music teach their children the beautiful lessons of the Word of God, learned through hymns that exalt his name, his love for us and remind us of his soon return to live a life eternal with our Creator, Sustainer and Redeemer.

In this book you will find easy piano arrangements of classic hymns that we all remember and love, as well as messages and coloring figures that children will love and will affirm the lyrics of these hymns in their hearts.

Diógenes Domínguez
8:14 Ministry

Hymns for Young Pianists

Contents

All Hail the Power of Jesus' Name

By Oliver Holden
Arr. Diógenes Domínguez

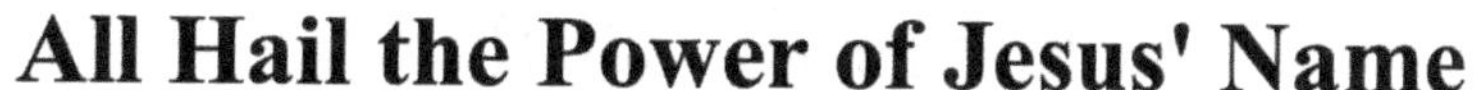

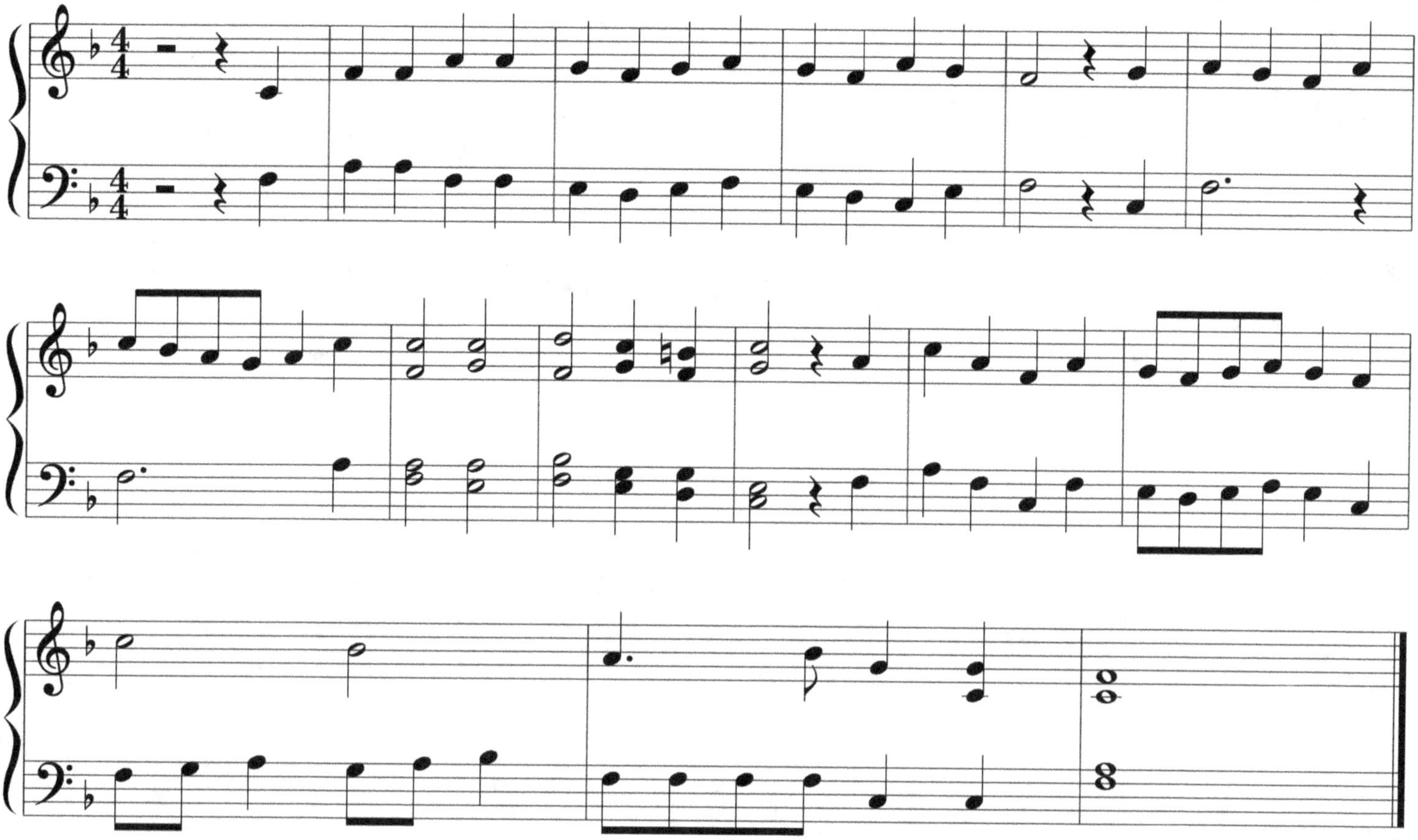

There's NO OTHER NAME like Jesus

Give Me the Bible

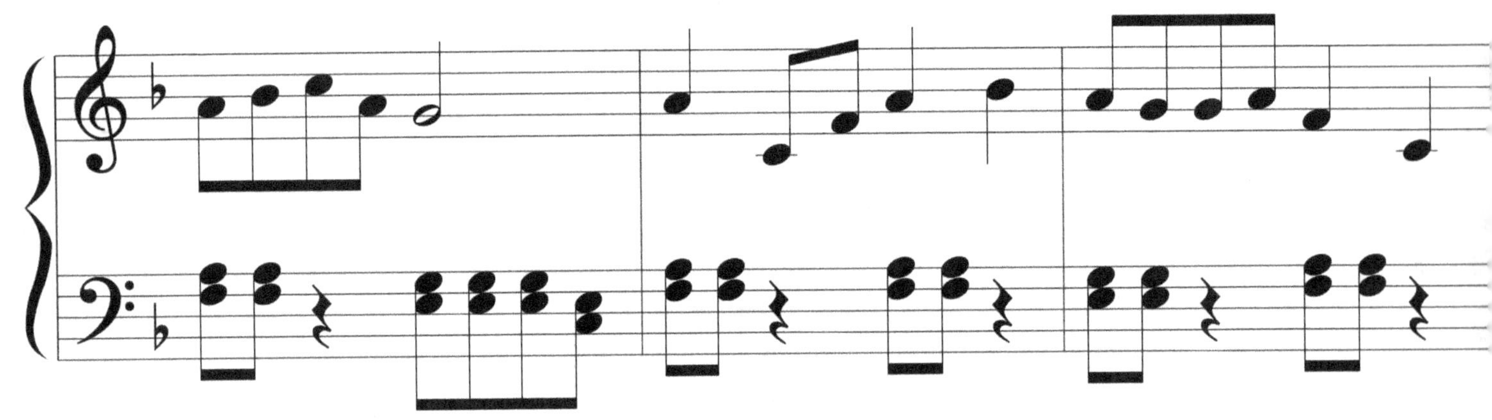

Fairest Lord Jesus

From Schlesische Volkslieder
Arr. Diógenes Domínguez

Jesus Shall Reign

By John Halton
Arr. Diógenes Domínguez

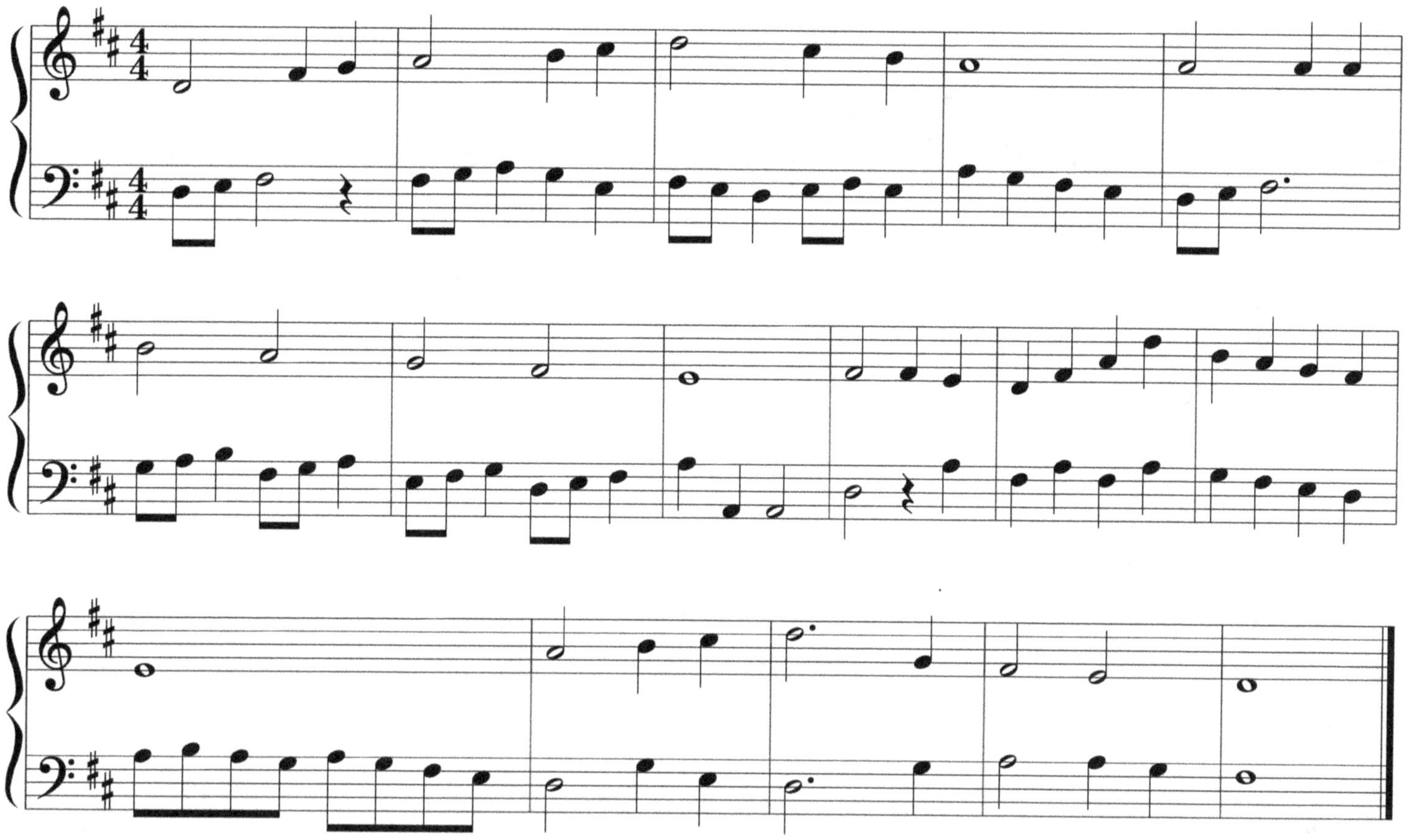

Jesus is King!

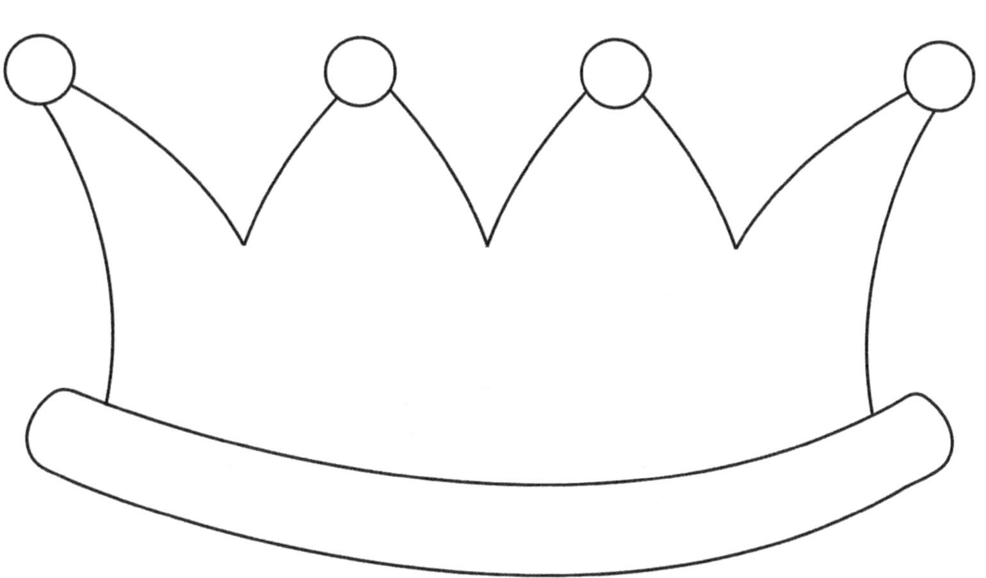

I Cannot Tell

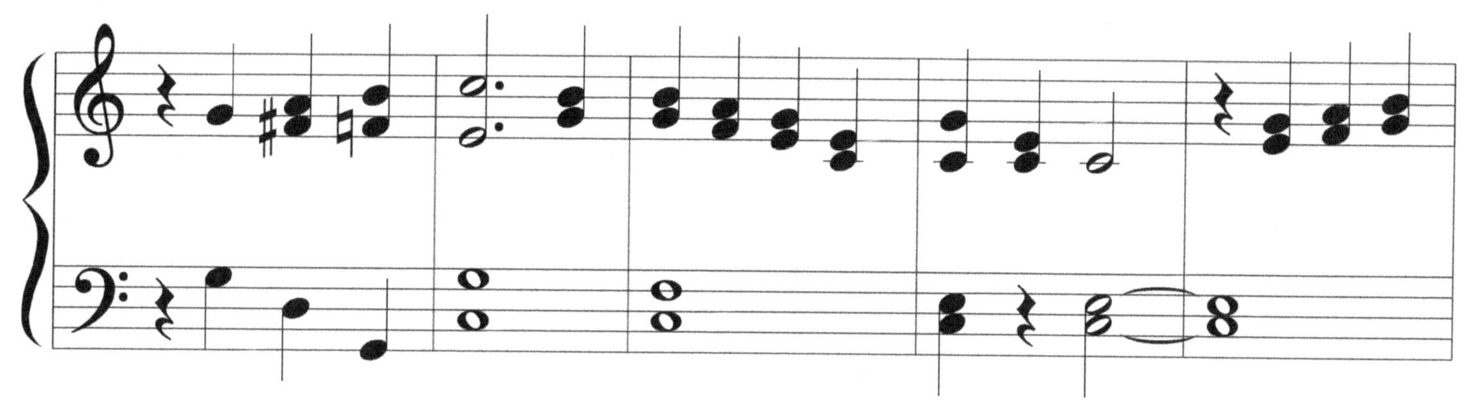

O, How I Love Jesus

19th Century American Melody
Arr. Diógenes Domínguez

Worthy, Worthy is the Lamb

Unknown Composer
Arr. Diógenes Domínguez

Praise Him! Praise Him!

By Chester G. Allen
Arr. Diógenes Domínguez

Rejoice, The Lord is King

By John Darwall
Arr. Diógenes Domínguez

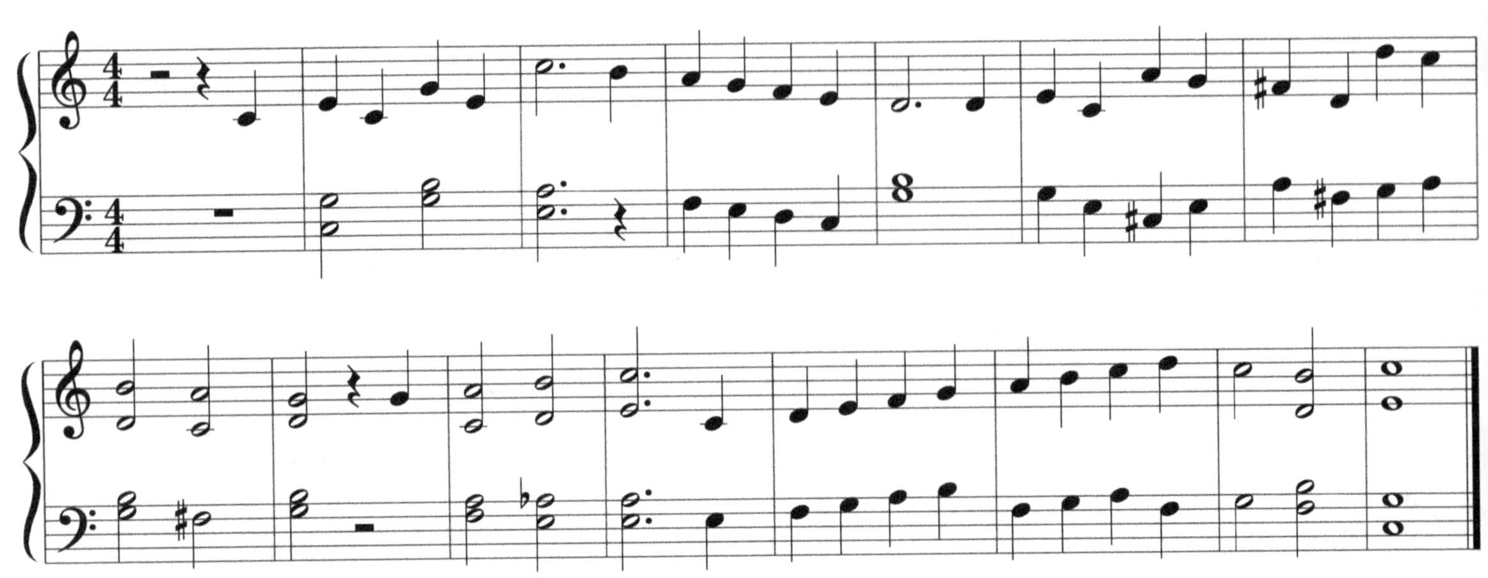

R-e-j-o-i-c-e!

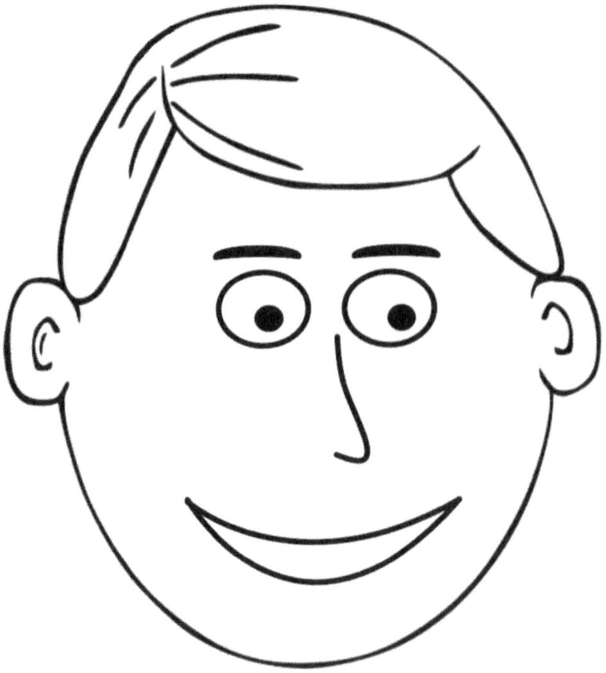

When He Cometh

By George F. Root
Arr. Diógenes Domínguez

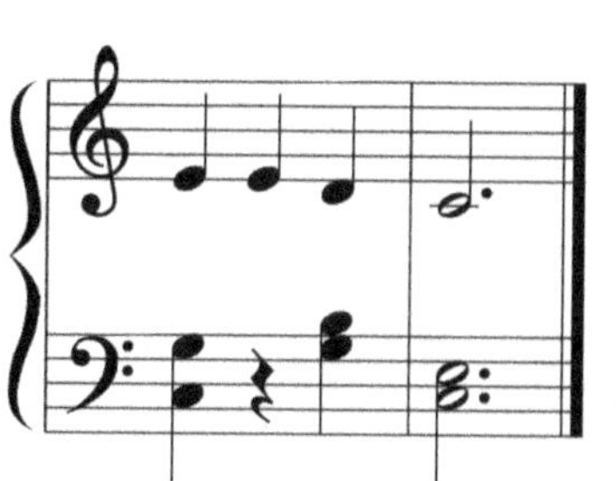

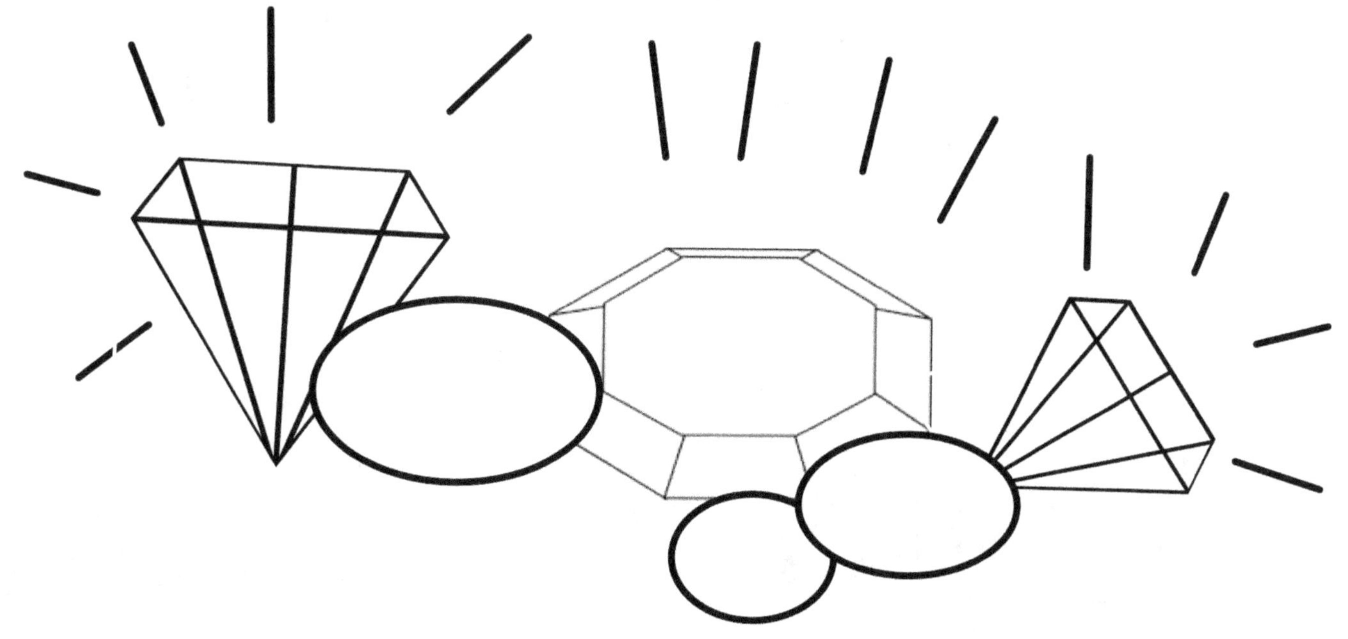

Abide with Me

By William H. Monk
Arr. Diógenes Domínguez

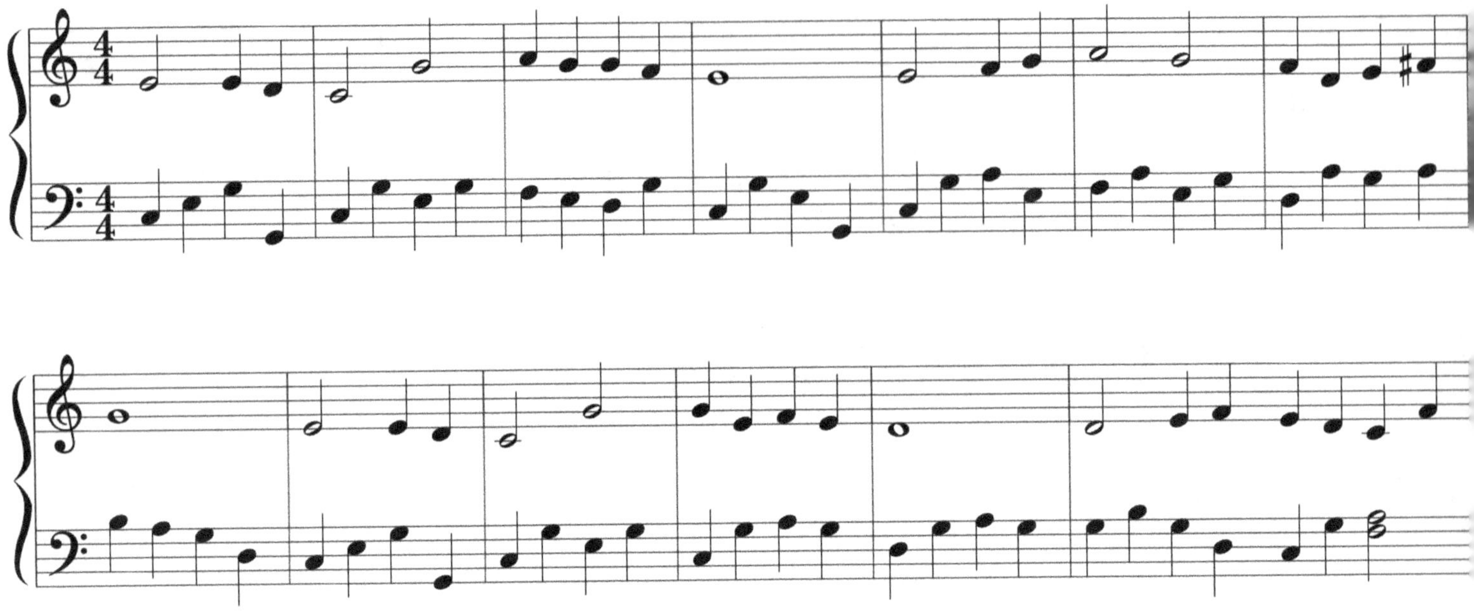

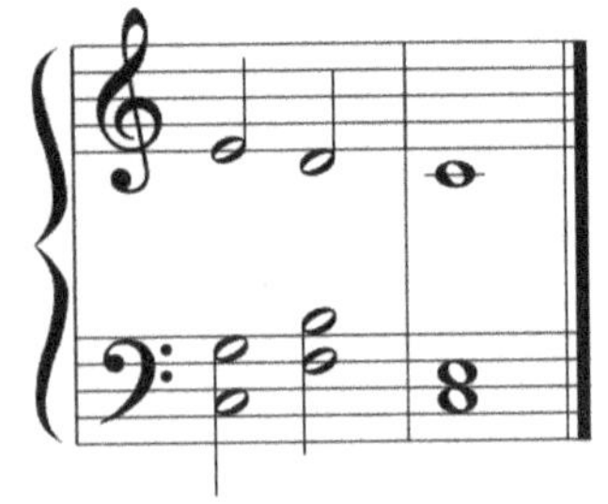

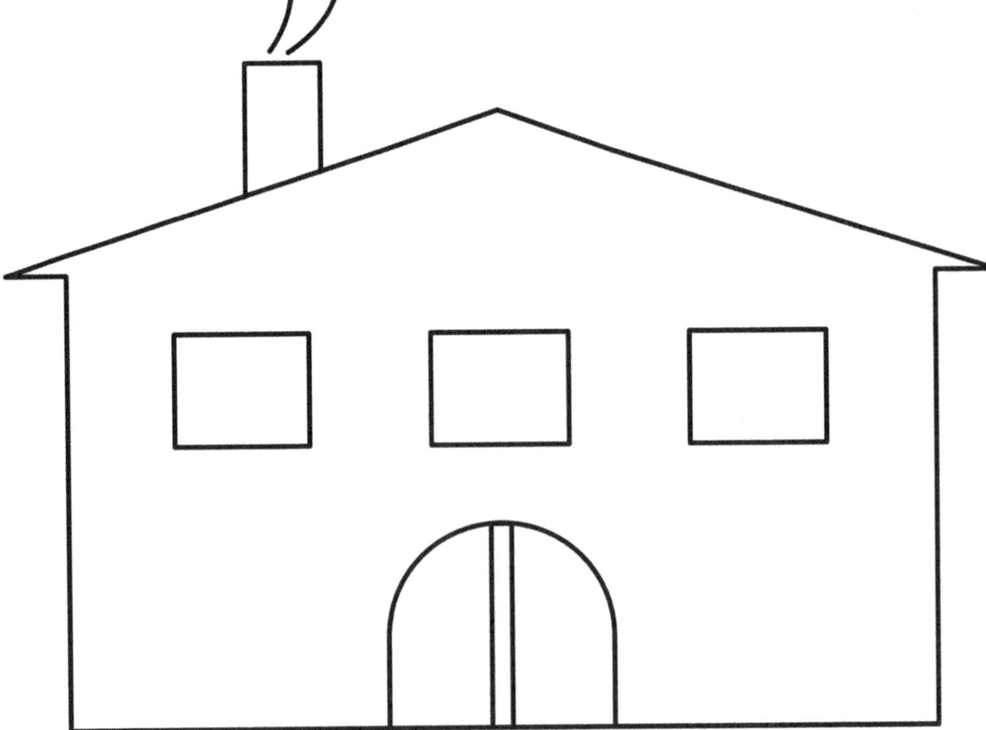

At Home with Jesus!

Amazing Grace

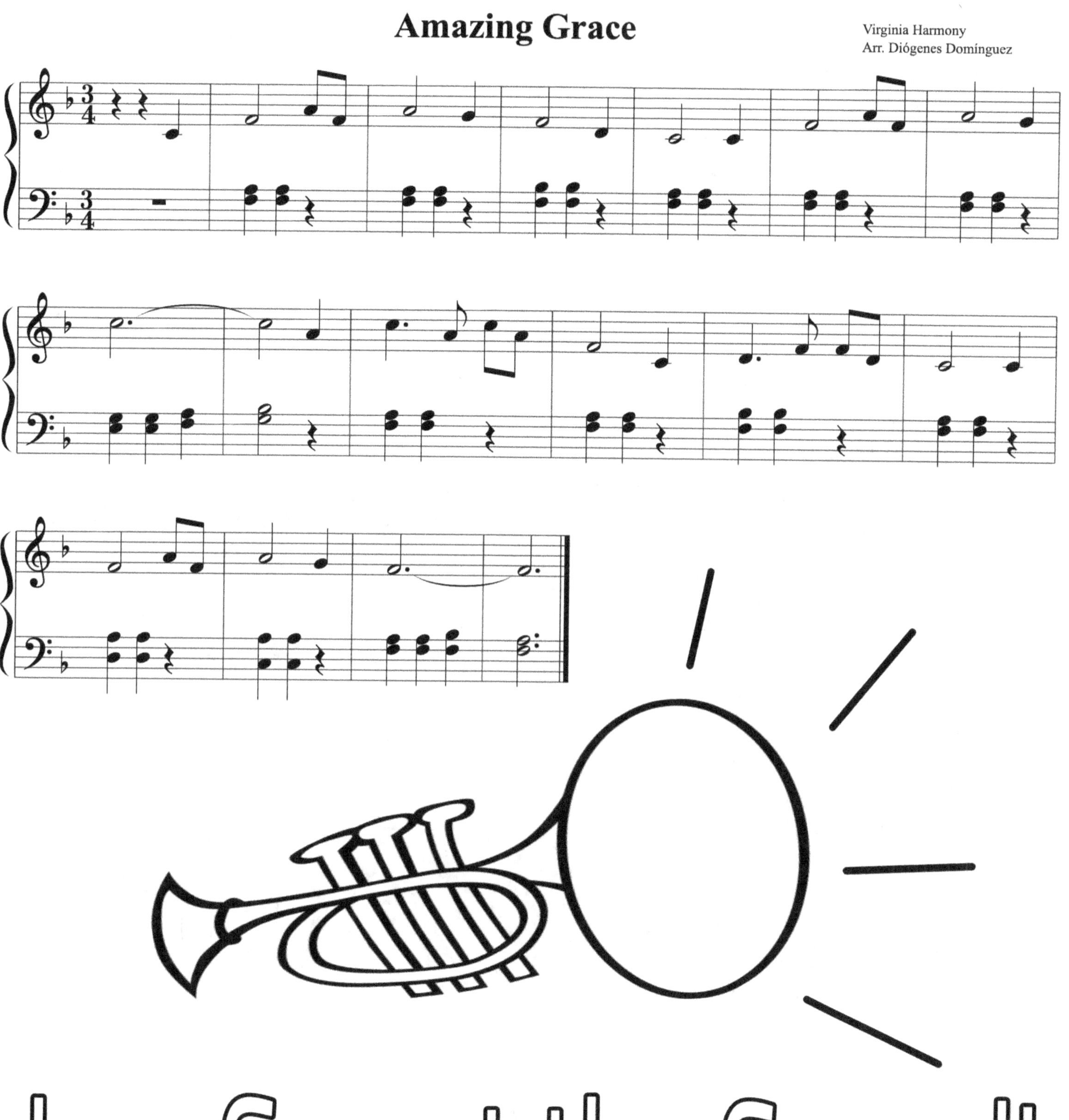

At the Cross

By Ralph E. Hudson
Arr. Diógenes Domínguez

God will Take Care of You

19

I Have a Joy, Joy, Joy

Arr. Diógenes Domínguez

Jesus Loves Me

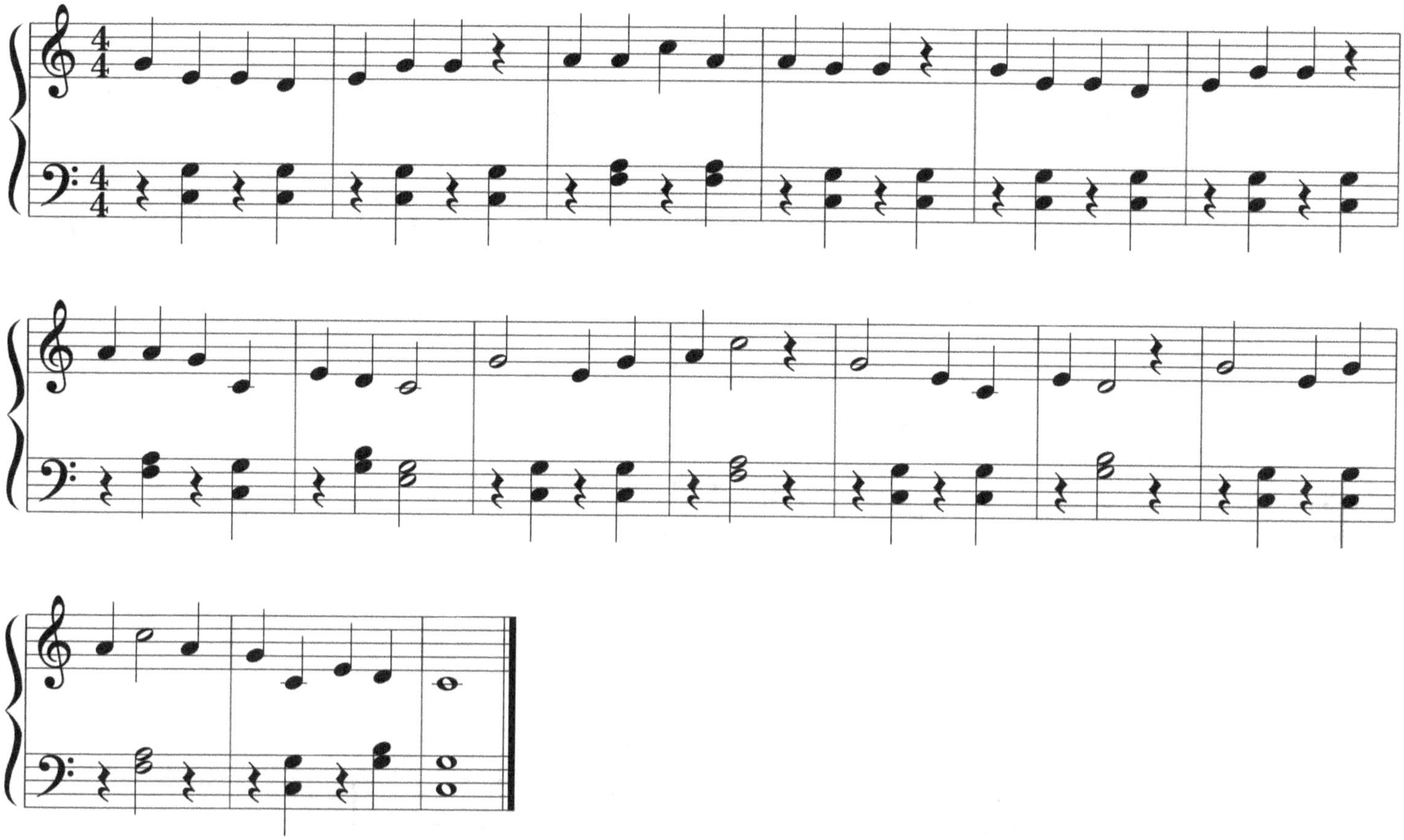

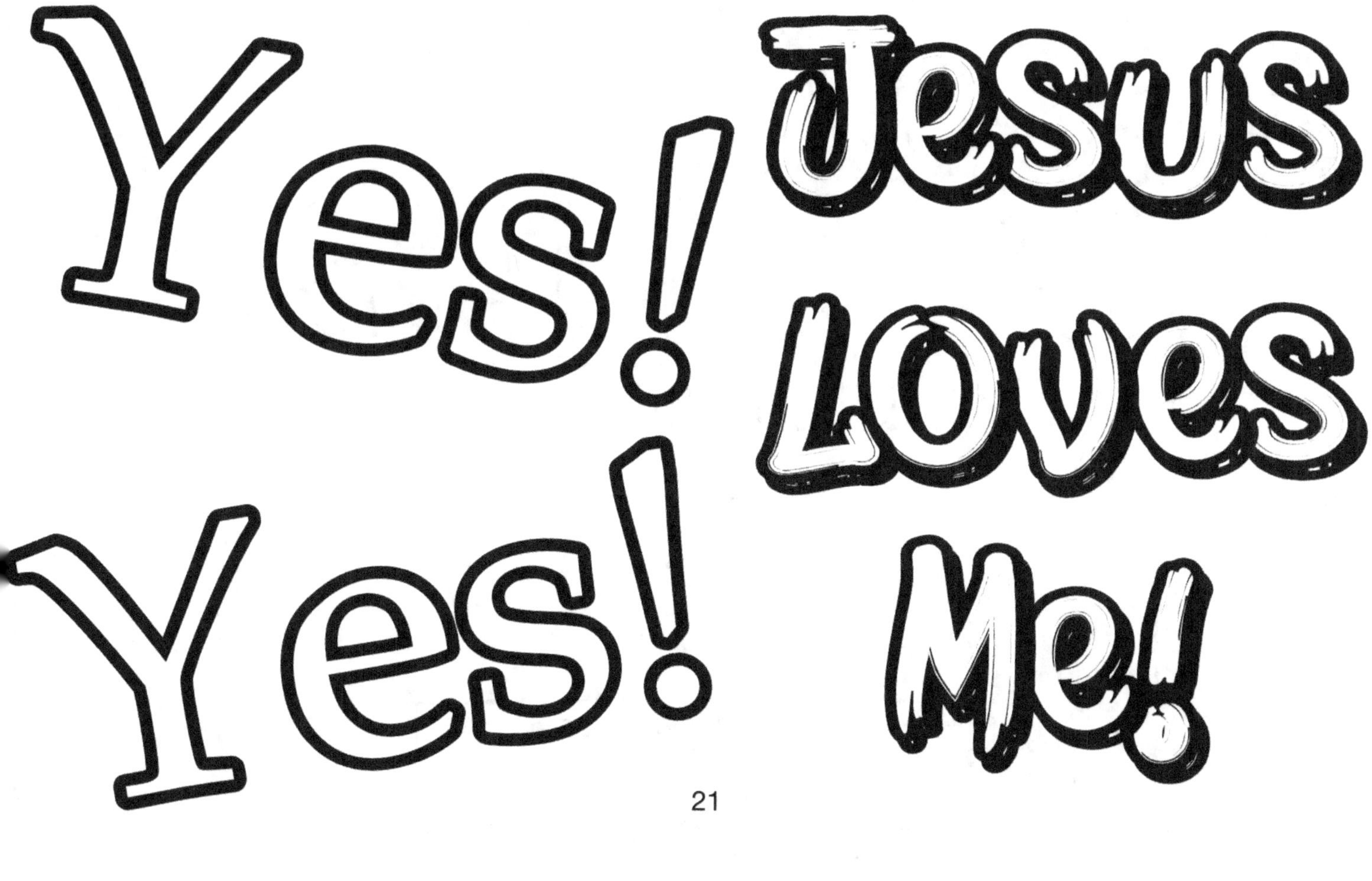

My Hope is Built on Nothing Less

O Worship the King

Our Shield and Defender

Ode to Joy

By Ludwig van Beethoven
Arr. Diógenes Domínguez

Joyful! Joyful!
We Adore Him

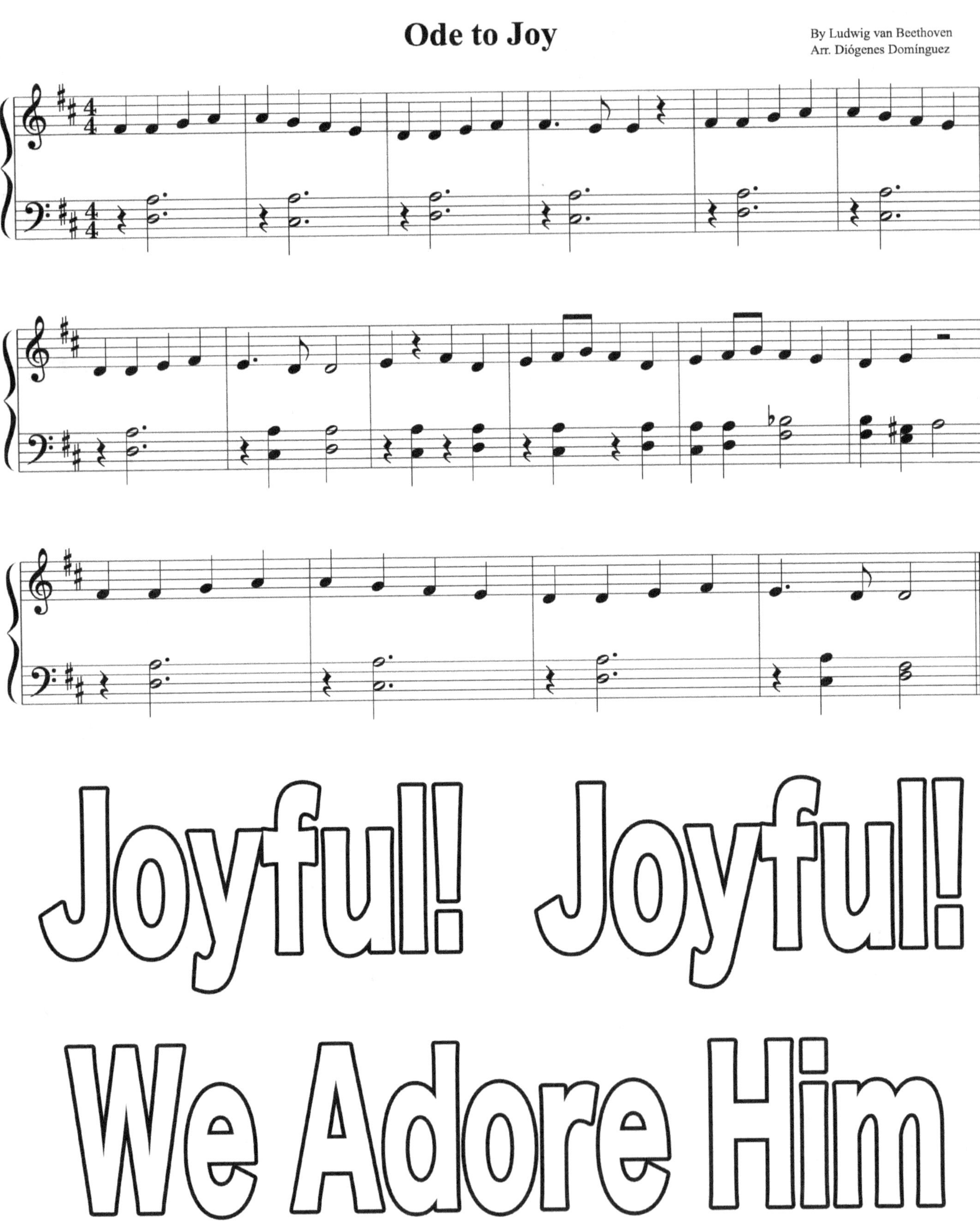

Rejoice, Ye Pure in Heart

By Arthur H. Messiter
Arr. Diógenes Domínguez

Take Time to be Holy

By George C. Stebbins
Arr. Diógenes Domínguez

This is My Father's World

By Franklin L. Sheppard
Arr. Diógenes Domínguez

27

What a Friend We have in Jesus

By Charles C. Converse
Arr. Diógenes Domínguez

Immortal, Invisible, God Only Wise

Welsh Melody
Arr.Diógenes Domínguez